A Glow of Emotions

Sad Glow's Journey to Happiness

Xanthe Asberry, M.A.

ISBN 979-8-89345-595-3 (paperback)
ISBN 979-8-89345-597-7 (digital)

Copyright © 2024 by Xanthe Asberry, M.A.

All rights reserved. No part of this publication may be reproduced, distributed, or transmitted in any form or by any means, including photocopying, recording, or other electronic or mechanical methods without the prior written permission of the publisher. For permission requests, solicit the publisher via the address below.

Christian Faith Publishing
832 Park Avenue
Meadville, PA 16335
www.christianfaithpublishing.com

Printed in the United States of America

This book is dedicated to the greatest school counselor, my mom, Harriett Davis, who served thousands of students with care and dedication throughout her 37-year career.

In the land of Glowville, where every glow shone brightly and cheerfully, there was one glow who felt differently. Sad Glow's light flickered dimly, and a shadow of sadness lingered over him. Tired of feeling blued, Sad Glow decided it was time for a change.

One night, as the stars twinkled above, Sad Glow set out on a daring adventure to find his lost happiness. Through meadows and forests, across rivers and mountains, Sad Glow journeyed, his light growing dimmer with each passing challenge.

Along the way, Sad Glow encountered different glows—some kind and helpful, others mischievous and unkind. Despite the obstacles and setbacks, Sad Glow persevered, determined to find the key to unlocking his inner light once more.

One day, as Sad Glow trudged wearily through a dark forest, a gentle glow approached him. It was Awareness Glow, a shimmering figure with a warm presence.

Awareness Glow: Hello, Sad Glow. I see that your light is dim. What troubles your heart?

Sad Glow: I feel so blued and lost. My light just won't shine brightly anymore.

Awareness Glow: It's okay to feel that way, Sad Glow. Remember, even the darkest night gives way to dawn. Let me share some steps with you to help find your light again.

LOVE
CARE
FRIENDS
GLOW
BEAUTY

Together, Sad Glow and Awareness Glow talked about seeking support, self-reflection, and focusing on positive solutions. As they journeyed together, Awareness Glow shared words of wisdom and encouragement, guiding Sad Glow through the challenges that lay ahead.

Through their conversations and shared experiences, Sad Glow began to see a glimmer of hope on the horizon. With each passing day, his light grew stronger, fueled by the newfound resilience and understanding he had gained. Finally, atop Hopeful Hill, as the sun rose over Glowville, Sad Glow's light sparkled brighter than ever before, illuminating the world with a radiant glow of happiness and self-acceptance.

Returning to Glowville as a transformed glow, Sad Glow shared his story with others, spreading a message of hope and courage to all who needed it.

And so Sad Glow's journey to happiness became a beacon of light for all in Glowville, a reminder that with the support of friends and the strength of self-belief, even the dimmest light can shine brightly once more.

The End

Dear Readers,

In the quiet corners of our hearts, sometimes a glow appears, a subtle radiance that speaks of the emotions we often shy away from—the beautiful, poignant hues of sadness. Today, we explore the Sad Glow, acknowledging its presence and finding solace in the shared experience.

Embracing the Sad Glow
(A Poem and Activity to Share)

Sad Glow here, feeling really blued,
So much has happened to spoil my mood.
Under the covers, I like to hide.
No light to shine, I've lost my pride.

This down feeling sticks like glue,
I miss my glimmer, my hopeful view.
When sadness comes, I just want to cry.
My friend Awareness Glow says there are
steps I should try.

I then seek support from those who care,
To share my feelings of despair.
I know just the group to meet my needs,
Mom, Dad, teacher, and counselor indeed.

They're concerned, empathetic, and caring too.
They always know just what to do.
In order to find the light in my tunnel of
hope, we talk about healthy ways to cope.

Imagery sparks a plan in my mind.
I'm now focused on the helping hand I'll find.

I self-reflect and ask myself, "How do I feel?"

I decide to stay solution-focused and let positivity heal.

Surrounding myself with happy friends
Helps my sadness reach its end.
My glow is back, I'm happy once more.
Awareness was right, I'm able to soar.

Though I may, at times, feel blued.
I have the skills to improve my mood.
I will stop and think, I will not hide.
I now have the tools to be my guide.

Activity: "Glowing Through Feelings" Creative Expression

Objective: To help students explore and express their feelings creatively while learning about coping strategies and seeking support.

Materials Needed

- Paper
- Coloring materials (markers, colored pencils, crayons)
- Glitter glue or glitter pens (optional)
- Scissors
- Glue
- Magazines or printed images for collage (optional)

Instructions:

1. Begin by reading the poem "Sad Glow" aloud to the students, emphasizing the emotions and coping strategies mentioned in the poem.

2. Discuss the importance of recognizing and expressing feelings, seeking support, and using healthy coping mechanisms when feeling sad or down.

3. Encourage students to reflect on a time they felt sad or down and how they coped with those feelings. Discuss the support systems they have in place or can reach out to for help.

4. Invite students to create a visual representation of their feelings and coping strategies using the materials provided. They can choose to create a drawing, a collage, or a combination of both.

5. Encourage students to use colors, images, and words to express their emotions and the steps they can take to feel better. They can incorporate elements from the poem or create their own original pieces inspired by the theme.

6. After the students have completed their artworks, invite them to share their creations with the class. Encourage them to explain the emotions depicted in their artwork and the coping strategies they have chosen to represent.

7. Facilitate a discussion about the different ways students cope with sadness and the importance of seeking support from others. Emphasize the message of the poem about finding light in times of darkness and using positivity to overcome challenges.

About the Author

 Xanthe Asberry is a dedicated educator and certified school counselor with over seventeen years of enriching experience in the field of education. By day, she passionately engages with students and stakeholders, fostering a positive and supportive learning environment. By night, Xanthe channels her creativity into crafting compelling, thought-provoking books that ignite self-awareness, instill hope, and encourage personal growth.

Residing in Tampa Bay, Florida, Xanthe shares her life with her loving husband and three delightful daughters. Through her writings, she aspires to leave a lasting impact on readers, inspiring them to embark on journeys of self-discovery and embrace the transformative power of hope and resilience.

Check out this author's other book:

www.ingramcontent.com/pod-product-compliance
Lightning Source LLC
Chambersburg PA
CBHW040157110726

48005CB00018B/2793